природа
(pryroda)
NATURE

дерево
(derevo)

tree

сонце
(sontse)

sun

озеро
(ozero)

lake

Гора
(hora)

mountain

МОГАЙН

LEARNING ENGLISH

FOR UCRAINIANS

вивчати англійську для українців

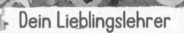

Dein Lieblingslehrer

table of contents

ЗМІСТ

Лісовий
(lisovyy)

forest

ФОРЕСТ

хмара
(khmara)

cloud

дощ
(doshch)

rain

лист
(lyst)

leaf

світ
(svit)

earth

місяць
(misyats')

moon

трава
(trava)

grass

квітка
(kvitka)

flower

зipка
(zirka)

star

планети
(planety)

planet

веселка
(veselka)

rainbow

море
(more)

sea

камінь (kamin') — stone

Вогонь (vohon') — fire

деревина (derevyna) — wood

небеса (nebesa) — sky

повітря
(povitrya)

air

вода
(voda)

water

Земля
(zemlya)

ground

сніг
(snih)

snow

вітер
(viter)

wind

пісок
(pisok)

sand

гілка
(hilka)

branch

троянда
(troyanda)

rose

туман
(tuman)

fog

Пляжний
(plyazhnyy)

beach

Острів
(Ostriv)

island

Пальма
(Pal'ma)

palm tree

Тепер твоя черга

Now it's your turn

камінь
(kamin')

stone

Вогонь
(vohon')

fire

деревина
(derevyna)

roof

небеса
(nebesa)

sky

дерево
(derevo)

tree

сонце
(sontse)

sun

озеро
(ozero)

Lake

Гора
(hora)

mountain

Їсти / Випити
(yisty) / (Vypyty)

FOOD

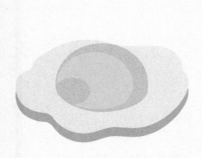

яблуко
(yabluko)

apple

торт
(tort)

cake

гамбургер
(hamburher)

hamburger

лимонад
(lymonad)

lemonade

Виноград  grapes
(Vynohrad)

макарони pasta
(makarony)

кола cola
(kola)

лимон lemon
(lymon)

спагетті 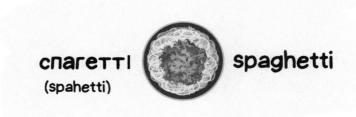 **spaghetti**
(spahetti)

апельсиновий сік **orange juice**
(apel'synovyy sik)

рис  **rice**
(rys)

курка **chicken**
(kurka)

картопля фрі fries
(kartoplya fri)

хліб  bread
(khlib)

кетчуп  ketchup
(ketchup)

цибуля  onion
(tsybulya)

багет
(bahet)

baguette

варення
(varennya)

jam

молоко
(moloko)

milk

чай
(chay)

tea

мед
(med)

honey

кави
(kavy)

coffee

тост
(tost)

toast

помідор
(pomidor)

tomato

яйце
(yaytse)

egg

сир
(syr)

cheese

огірок
(ohirok)

cucumber

Пальма
(kakao)

hot chocolate

овочі
(ovochi)

vegetables

фрукти
(frukty)

fruit

морква
(morkva)

carrot

брокколі
(brokkoli)

broccoli

шоколад  chocolate
(shokolad)

морозиво ice cream
(morozyvo)

солодкий sweet
(solodkyy)

майонез mayonnaise
(mayonez)

НІЖ
(nizh)

knife

КНАЙФ

вилка
(vylka)

fork

furk

Тарілка
(Tarilka)

plate

ложка
(lozhka)

spoon

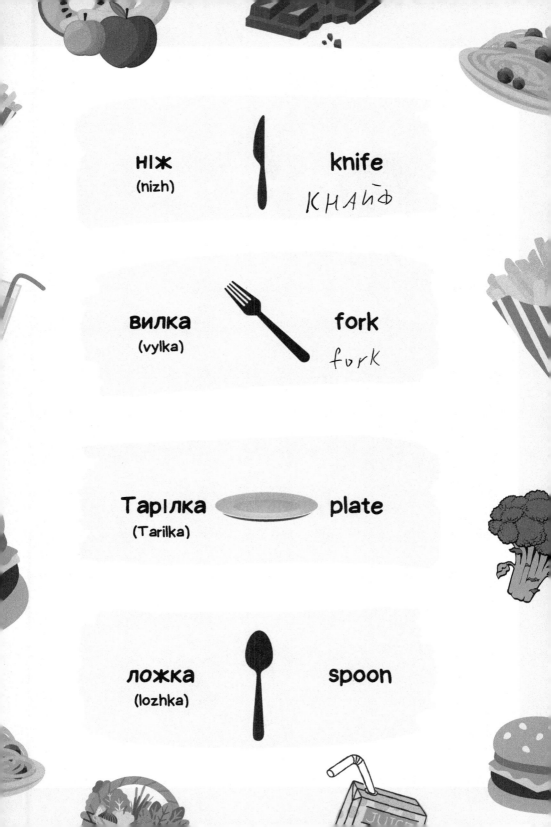

Тепер твоя черга

Now it's your turn

COFFEE

спагетті 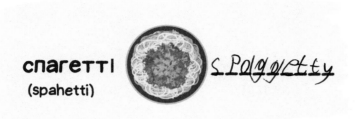 S P*a*g*e*tt*y*
(spahetti)

апельсиновий сік  *juice*
(apel'synovyy sik) ~~orangejuice~~

рис  *rise*
(rys)

курка  *chicken*
(kurka)

яйце
(yaytse)

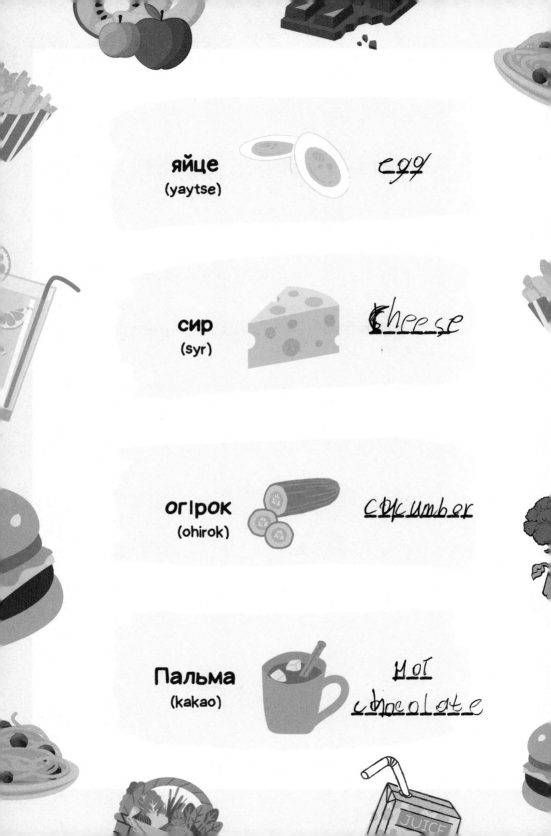

egg

сир
(syr)

cheese

огірок
(ohirok)

cucumber

Пальма
(kakao)

hot chocolate

Вдома
(Vdoma)
AT HOME

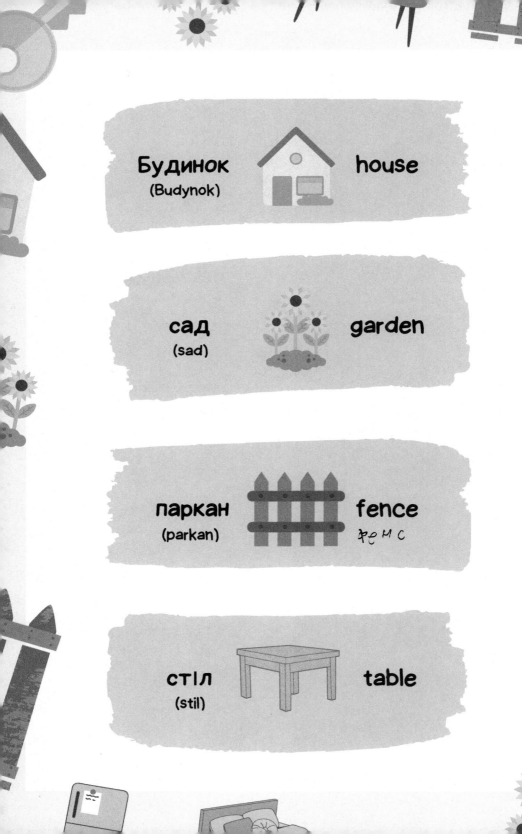

Будинок
(Budynok)

house

сад
(sad)

garden

паркан
(parkan)

fence

стіл
(stil)

table

стілець
(stilets')

chair

диван
dyvan

couch

подушка
(podushka)

pillow

ложка
(lizhko)

bed

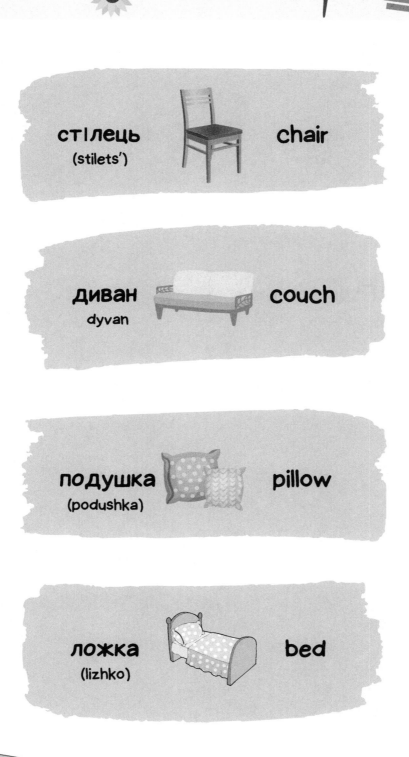

крісло
(krislo)

armchair

Підодіяльник
(Pidodiyal'nyk)

duvet

шафи
(shafy)

cabinet

лампа
(lampa)

lamp

телевізор
(televizor)

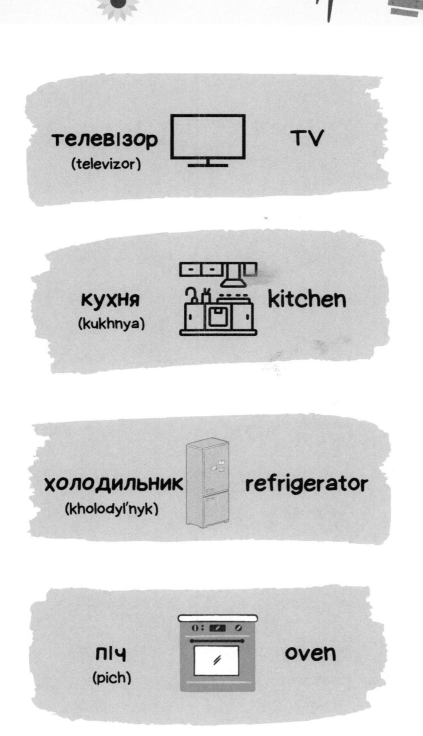

TV

кухня
(kukhnya)

kitchen

холодильник
(kholodyl'nyk)

refrigerator

піч
(pich)

oven

плита **stovetop**
plyta

ящик  **drawer**
(yashchyk)

килим carpet
(kylym)

опалення 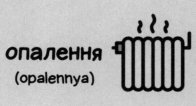 **heater**
(opalennya)

душ
(dush)

shower

ванна
(vanna)

bath

Туалет
(Tualet)

toilet

дверI
(dveri)

door

ключ
(klyuch)

key

Скло
(Sklo)

glass

ваза
(vaza)

vase

Сміттєвий бак
(Smittyevyy bak)

tashcan

гардероб
(harderob)

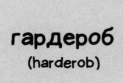

wardrobe

вікно
(vikno)

window

завіса
(zavisa)

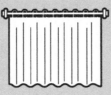

curtain

сходи
(skhody)

stairway

Тепер твоя черга

Now it's your turn

стілець
(stilets')

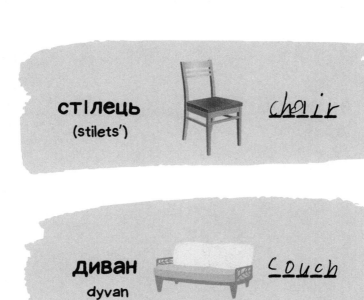

chair

диван
dyvan

couch

подушка
(podushka)

pillow

ложка
(lizhko)

bed

гардероб
(harderob)

_____

вікно
(vikno)

window

завіса
(zavisa)

curtain

сходи
(skhody)

stairway

душ
(dush)

shower

ванна
(vanna)

bath

Туалет
(Tualet)

toilet

дверı
(dveri)

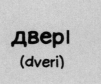

door

тварини
(tvaryny)

ANIMALS

собака
(sobaka)

dog

кіт
(kit)

cat

миша
(mysha)

mouse

слон
(slon)

elephant

жираф
(zhyraf)

giraffe

жаба
(zhaba)

frog

кінь
(kin')

horse

кролик
(krolyk)

rabbit

хом'яка
(khom'yaka)

hamster

павук
(pavuk)

spider

лисиця
(lysytsya)

fox

Їжачок
(Yizhachok)

hedgehog

птах
(ptakh)

bird

пінгвін
(pinhvin)

penguin

папуга
(papuha)

parrot

фламінго
(flaminho)

flamingo

свиня
(svynya)

pig

зебра
(zebra)

zebra

корова
(korova)

cow

вівці
(vivtsi)

sheep

Змія
(Zmiya)

snake

метелик
metelyk

butterfly

хробак
(khrobak)

worm

Лев
(Lev)

lion

ведмідь
(vedmid')

bear

мураха
(murakha)

ant

носоріг
(nosorih)

rhino

курка
(kurka)

chicken

Тепер твоя черга

Now it's your turn

ведмідь
(vedmid')

Bear

мураха
(murakha)
ant

носоріг
(nosorih)
rhino

курка
(kurka)
chicken

жираф
(zhyraf)

girrafe

жаба
(zhaba)

frog

кінь
(kin')

tours

кролик
(krolyk)

rabbit

cIMˡⁱ
(sim'yi)

FAMILY

батько
(bat'ko)

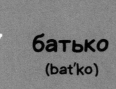

dad

мати
maty

mum

син
(syn)

son

дочка
(dochka)

daughter

ДЯДЬКО
(dyad'ko)

uncle

а́нкл

ТІТКА
(titka)

aunt

ДІдусь
(Didus')

grandpa

бабуся
(babusya)

granny

брати
(braty)

brother

сестра
(sestra)

sister

бабуся і дідусь
(babusya i didus')

grandparents

батьків
(bat'kiv)

parents

дитини
(dytyny)

child

немовля
(nemovlya)

baby

чоловік
(cholovik)

man

жінка
(zhinka)

woman

Тепер твоя черга

Now it's your turn

батько
(bat'ko)

dad

мати
maty

mum

син
(syn)

son

дочка
(dochka)

dbyghter
~~douther~~

ДИТИНИ
(dytyny)

child

НЕМОВЛЯ
(nemovlya)

BABY

ЧОЛОВІК
(cholovik)

man

ЖІНКА
(zhinka)

women

школу
(shkolu)

SCHOOL

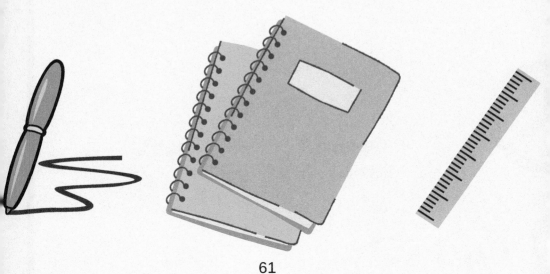

дошка
(doshka)

blackboard

крейда
(kreyda)

chalk

Учитель
(Uchytel')

teacher

учнів
(uchniv)

pupils

директора
(dyrektora)

principal

зошит
(zoshyt)

notebook

лінійка
(liniyka)

ruler

ранець
(ranets')

backpack

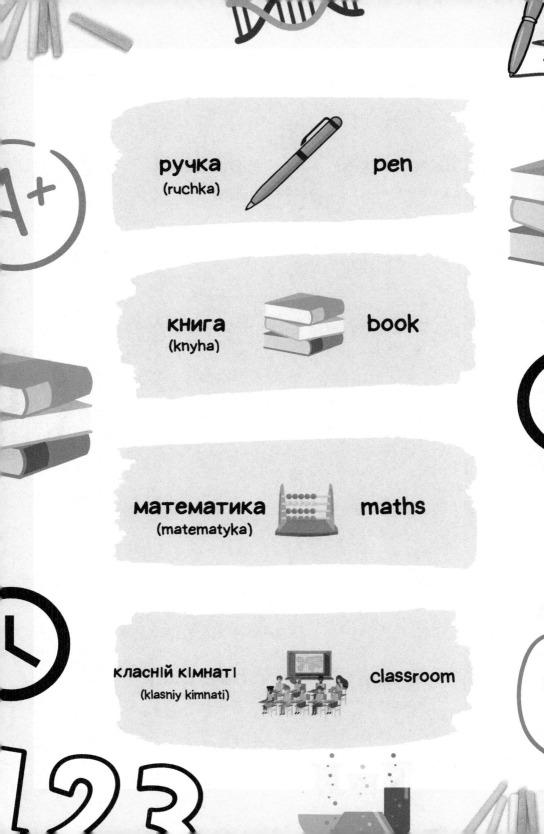

ручка
(ruchka)
pen

книга
(knyha)
book

математика
(matematyka)
maths

класній кімнаті
(klasniy kimnati)
classroom

хімія
(khimiya)

chemistry

біології
(biolohiyi)

biology

історія
(istoriya)

history

німецька
(nimets'ka)

German

англійська 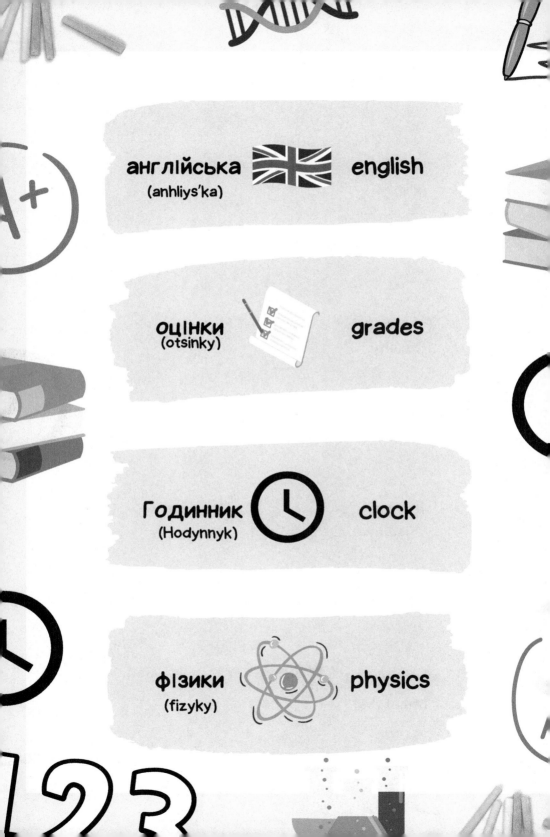 **english**
(anhliys'ka)

оцінки **grades**
(otsinky)

Годинник **clock**
(Hodynnyk)

фізики **physics**
(fizyky)

нульовий (nul'ovyy)	0	Zero
один (odyn)	1	one
два (dva)	2	two
Три (Try)	3	three

Чотири
(Chotyry) — **4** — four

п'ять
(p'yat') — **5** — five

шість
(shist') — **6** — six

cім
(sim) — **7** — seven

вісім
(visim)

8

eight

дев'ять
(dev'yat')

9

nine

циліндр
(tsylindr)

cylinder

коло
(kolo)

circle

піраміда **pyramid**
(piramida)

Майдан **square**
(Maydan)

прямокутник **rectangle**
(pryamokutnyk)

трикутник **triangle**
(trykutnyk)

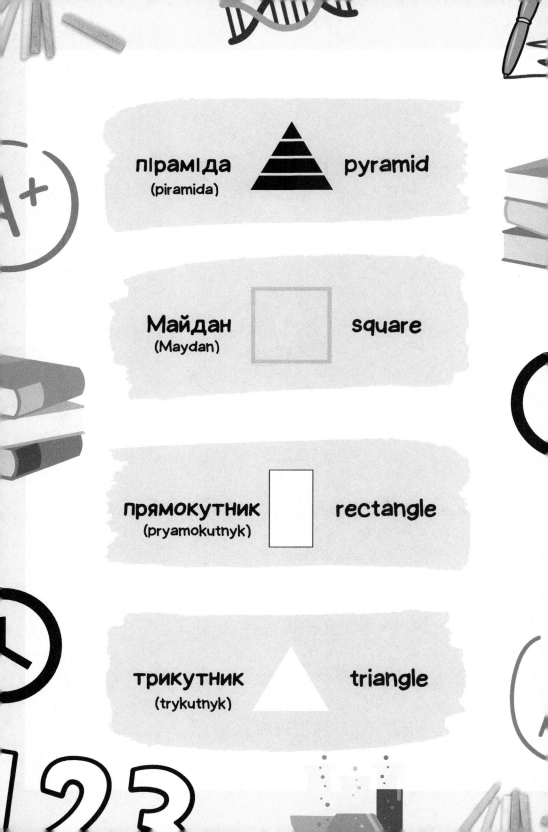

Тепер твоя черга

Now it's your turn

нульовий
(nul'ovyy)

0

z_ _ _ _

один
(odyn)

1

_ _ _ _

два
(dva)

2

_ _ _ _

Три
(Try)

3

_ _ _ _ _

піраміда
(piramida)

pyramid

Майдан
(Maydan)

square

прямокутник
(pryamokutnyk)

rectangle

трикутник
(trykutnyk)

triangle

ДОЗВІ́ЛЛЯ
(dozvillya)

LEISURE

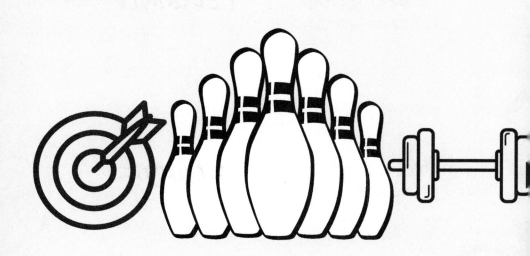

велосипед  bicycle
(velosyped)

футбол soccer
(futbol)

баскетбол basketball
(basketbol)

бадмінтон badminton
(badminton)

волейбол
(voleybol)
volleyball ✓

бігун
(bihun)
jogger ○

фітнес
(fitnes)
fitness ✓

басейн
(baseyn)
swimming pool ✓

боулінг
(boulinh)

bowling

дартс
(dart·s)

darts

теніс
(tenis)

tennis

настільний теніс
(nastil'nyy tenis)

table tennis

Тепер твоя черга

Now it's your turn

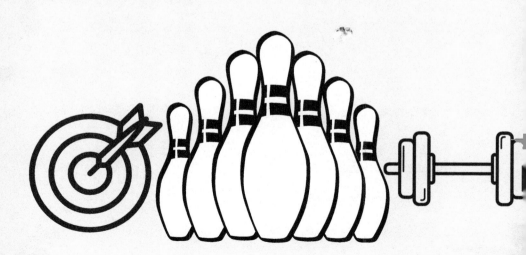

велосипед
(velosyped)

 bicycle

футбол
(futbol)

 *soccer*

баскетбол
(basketbol)

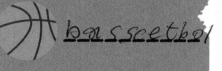 *basscetbol*

бадмінтон
(badminton)

 b_adminton

технологїі
(tekhnolohiyi)

TECHNOLOGY

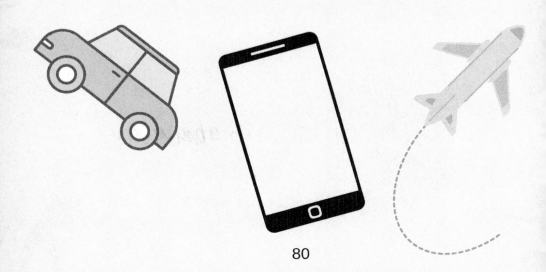

комп'ютер
(komp'yuter)
computer

ноутбук
(noutbuk)
laptop

мікрофон
(mikrofon)
microphone

клавіатуру
(klaviaturu)
keyboard

Інтернет
(Internet)

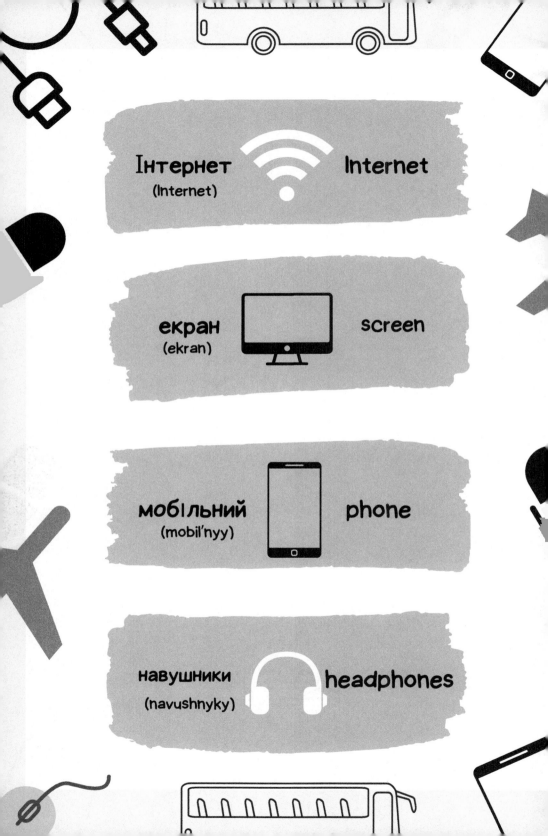

Internet

екран
(ekran)

screen

мобільний
(mobil'nyy)

phone

навушники
(navushnyky)

headphones

миша
(mysha)

mouse

кабель
(kabel')

cable

розетка
(rozetka)

socket

динамік
(dynamik)

speaker

автомобільний
(avtomobil'nyy)

car

скутер
(skuter)

scooter

літак
(litak)

plane

гелікоптер
(helikopter)

helicopter

автобус 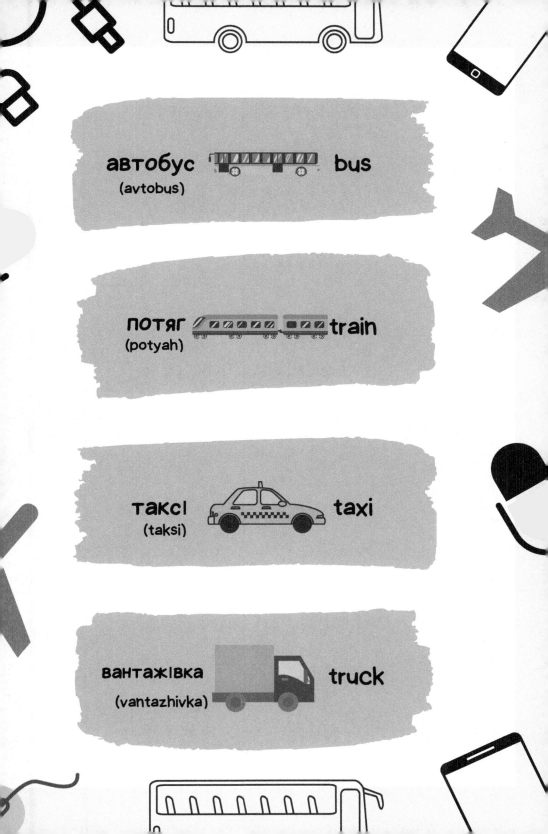 bus
(avtobus)

потяг train
(potyah)

таксі taxi
(taksi)

вантажівка truck
(vantazhivka)

Тепер твоя черга

Now it's your turn

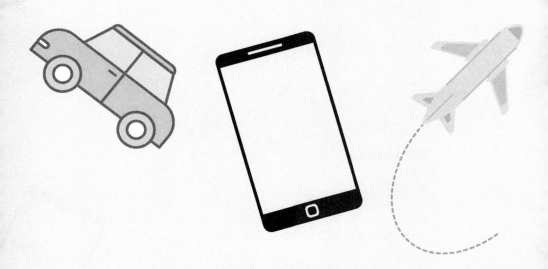

автомобільний
(avtomobil'nyy)  _cut_

скутер
(skuter) _scooter_

літак
(litak) _plane_

гелікоптер
(helikopter) _helicopter_

Інтернет
(Internet)

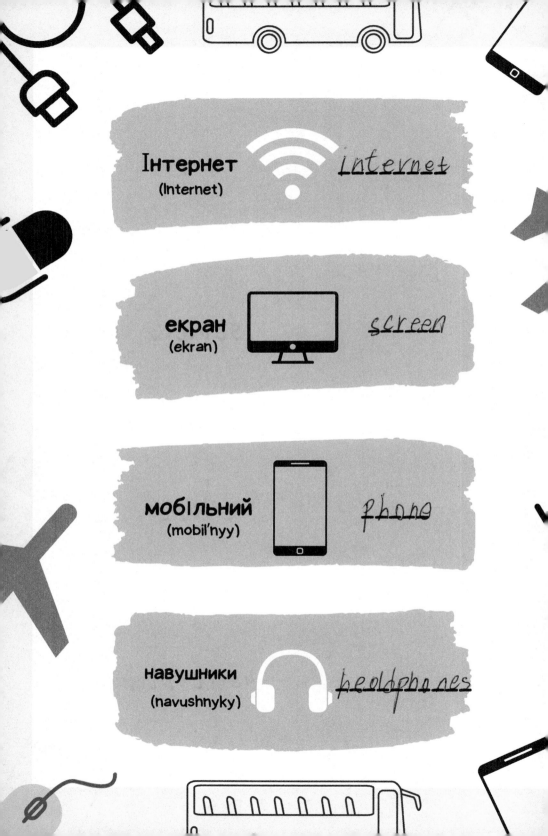

internet

екран
(ekran)

screen

мобільний
(mobil'nyy)

phone

навушники
(navushnyky)

headphones

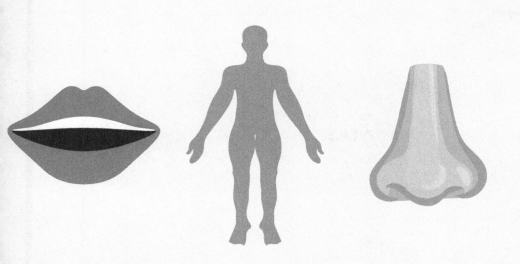

ТІЛО
(tilo)

BODY

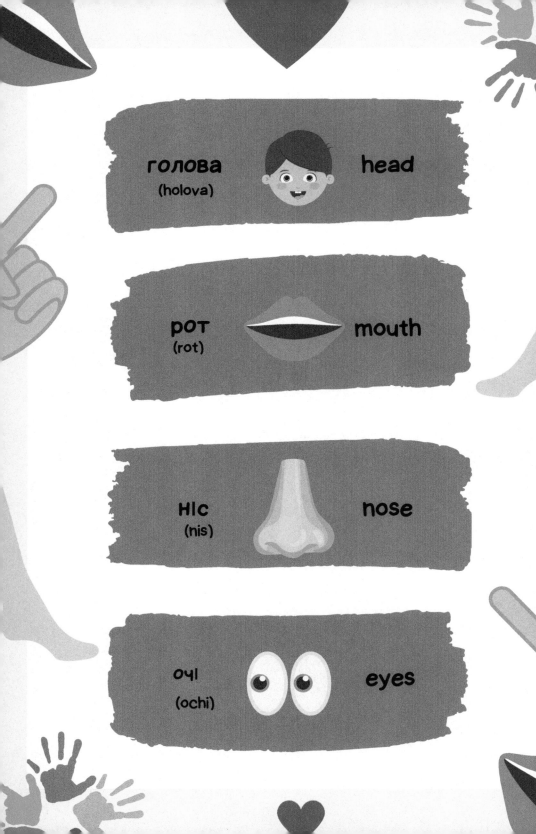

голова
(holova)

head

рот
(rot)

mouth

ніс
(nis)

nose

очі
(ochi)

eyes

вуха
(vukha)

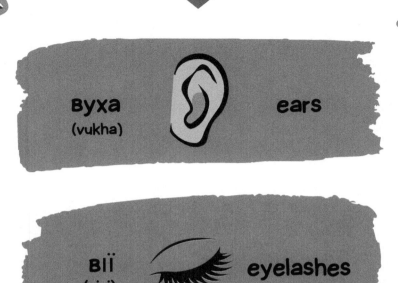

ears

вії
(viyi)

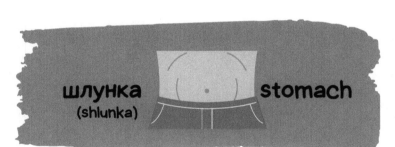

eyelashes

шлунка
(shlunka)

stomach

рухатися
(rukhatysya)

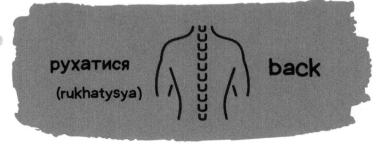

back

волосся
(volossya)

hair

бідний
(bidnyy)

arms

пальцем
(pal'tsem)

finger

рука
(ruka)

hand

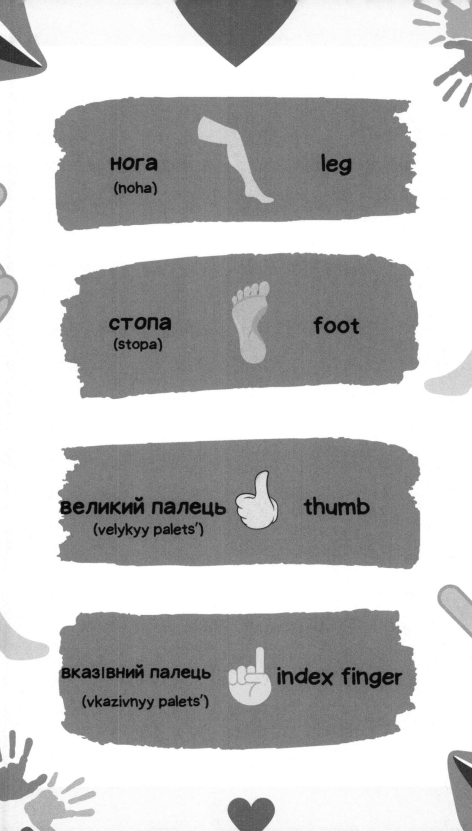

нога
(noha)

leg

стопа
(stopa)

foot

великий палець
(velykyy palets')

thumb

вказівний палець
(vkazivnyy palets')

index finger

середнiй палець middle finger
(s:eredniy palets')

безiменний палець  ring finger
(bezimennyy palets')

мiзинець pinkie finger
(mizynets')

зуби teeth
(zuby)

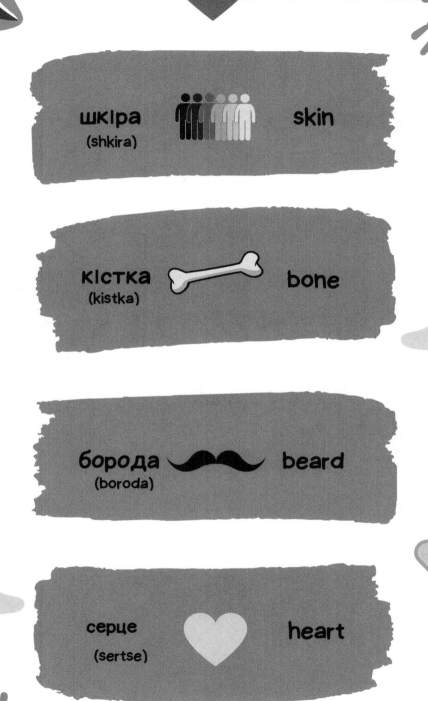

шкіра (shkira) — skin

кістка (kistka) — bone

борода (boroda) — beard

серце (sertse) — heart

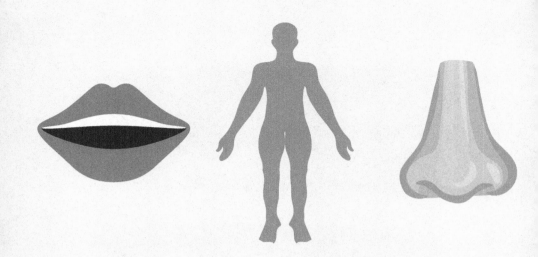

Тепер твоя черга

Now it's your turn

нога
(noha)

leg

стопа
(stopa)

foot

великий палець
(velykyy palets')

thumb

вказівний палець
(vkazivnyy palets')

index finger

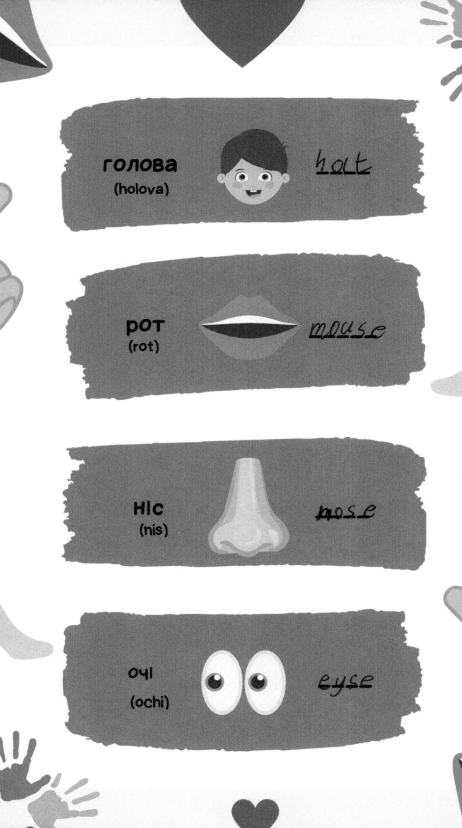

голова
(holova)

hat

рот
(rot)

mouse

ніс
(nis)

nose

очі
(ochi)

eyse

I am, finish! ♡

Imprint

Printed in Great Britain
by Amazon

78989189R00059